# Why do chimps kiss?

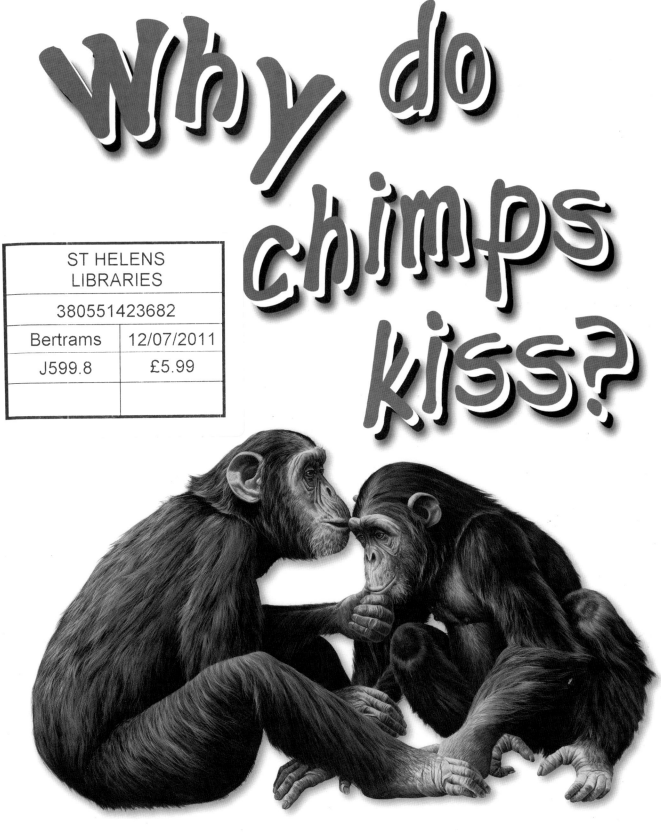

camilla de la Bedoyere

First published in 2011 by Miles Kelly Publishing Ltd
Harding's Barn, Bardfield End Green, Thaxted,
Essex, CM6 3PX, UK

Copyright © Miles Kelly Publishing Ltd 2011

2 4 6 8 10 9 7 5 3 1

Publishing Director  Belinda Gallagher
Creative Director  Jo Cowan
Editorial Director  Rosie McGuire
Editor  Sarah Parkin
Volume Designer  Phil Morash at Fineline Studios
Cover Designer  Kayleigh Allen
Image Manager  Liberty Newton
Indexer  Gill Lee
Production Manager  Elizabeth Collins
Reprographics  Anthony Cambray, Stephan Davis

ISBN 978-1-84810-460-0

Printed in China

British Library Cataloguing-in-Publication Data

A catalogue record for this book is
available from the British Library

**ACKNOWLEDGEMENTS**
The publishers would like to thank the following
artists who have contributed to this book:

Ian Jackson (cover), Mike Foster (character cartoons)
All other artwork from the Miles Kelly Artwork Bank

The publishers would like to thank the following
sources for the use of their photographs:
**FLPA** 13 Pete Oxford/Minden Pictures;
18 Cyril Ruoso/Minden Pictures
**iStockphoto.com** 6 Robert Churchill; 28 Matthew Okimi
**Moviestore Collection** 25 Walt Disney Productions
**Shutterstock.com** 5 javarman; 7 Vladimir Wrangel;
9 Sara Robinson; 14 Vitaly Titov & Maria Sidelnikova;
21 Animal; 22 Mike Price

Every effort has been made to acknowledge the
source and copyright holder of each picture.
Miles Kelly Publishing apologises for any unintentional
errors or omissions.

Made with paper from a sustainable forest

www.mileskelly.net
info@mileskelly.net

www.factsforprojects.com

Self-publish your
children's book

buddingpress.co.uk

# Contents

# what is a primate?

**Monkeys and apes are primates.** They have big brains and are very clever. Most primates are furry. They have hands with thumbs and fingernails. Humans are primates too.

Spider monkeys

## cry baby!

Bushbabies are noisy primates that live in forests. When they make loud calls to each other, they sound like crying babies.

## Spell

How many words can you make using the letters in the word PRIMATE?

## Are gorillas scary?

Gorillas are usually gentle animals. However they can be very fierce if they have to protect their families. Males can die fighting to save their young.

## Do monkeys and apes have tails?

Monkeys have tails, but apes don't. Tails help monkeys to climb and keep their balance. Apes are usually larger than monkeys and they also have bigger brains. Gorillas, chimpanzees (chimps), bonobos, orang-utans, gibbons and humans are apes.

Orang-utan

5

# Do primates stay awake all night?

**Nocturnal primates do!** Animals that are nocturnal sleep during the day and wake up at sunset. Tarsiers have big eyes to help them see in the dark. They can turn their heads right round, so they can see what's behind them.

Tarsier

# Do bonobos like to play?

Bonobos love to play! Some bonobos living in a zoo play their own game of 'blind man's bluff'! They cover their eyes and try to walk without bumping into things.

## Play

Ask a grown-up to help you set up a game of 'blind man's bluff' with your friends.

# Which lemur has a stripy tail?

Ring-tailed lemurs have long, bushy tails with black-and-white stripes. The males have smelly tails, and when they fight they wave them at each other.

Ring-tailed lemur

## Hold tight!

Lemurs run and jump through trees. Babies have to grip tightly to their mothers' fur so they don't fall off!

# Why do chimps lick sticks?

**Because they get covered with juicy termites!** Chimps poke sticks into big termite nests. The insects swarm over the sticks, which the chimps then pull out so they can lick up the tasty termites.

Chimps →

## Sign

Use the Internet to discover how to sign for 'drink' and 'thank you'.

## Greedy monkey!

Barbary macaques have large cheek pouches. When they find food, they stuff it into their pouches and save it for later.

## Do chimps like to chatter?

Some do! A chimp called Washoe learnt how to use sign language to talk. She used her hands to make signs for lots of words, such as 'drink' and 'food'.

Squirrel monkey

## Why do monkeys sleep in trees?

Monkeys can hide in a tree's branches, so they feel safer in trees than on the ground. Animals that want to eat other animals are called predators. The predators of squirrel monkeys include eagles, baboons and prickly porcupines.

# Do apes love their mums?

**Yes!** All ape babies need their mums to look after them, but orang-utan babies need their mums the most. They stay with their mothers until they are eight years old. That's longer than any other primate, apart from humans.

Orang-utan and baby

# Why does an aye-aye have a long finger?

An aye-aye has a long finger to get to tasty grubs. These little primates tap trees with their fingers. If they hear a grub moving inside, they make a hole and pull it out with their extra-long middle finger.

Aye-aye

## What a racket!

Some mangabeys make a 'honk-bark' noise. Others 'whoop' to call each other and make a 'gobble' sound to say who they are.

# Why do orang-utans climb trees?

Orang-utans climb trees to play amongst the branches, to find fruit to eat and to stay safe. Predators such as tigers, leopards and crocodiles hunt orang-utans.

## Make

Who looks after you? Create them a beautiful card to say 'thank you'.

# Why do chimps kiss?

**Chimps can be very loving to members of their family.** They like to sit together and kiss, stroke and groom each other. If chimps are annoyed they cough, but if they are very angry they bark, cry and scream.

Chimps

# Do primates use tools?

Some primates use tools to help them get food. Capuchin monkeys use heavy rocks to crack open hard nuts. Apes can use tools too, and they even teach each other how to use rocks to open nuts.

Brown capuchin

## Time for change!

People love to watch chimps. Sadly, some chimps are taken from the wild to be put in zoos or even sold as pets.

## Discover

Use books and the Internet to find other animals that use tools.

# When do baboons show off?

Male baboons love to show off when there are females about. They swagger around to show off their big muscles, long fangs and fine fur.

# Do primates help forests to grow?

**Yes they do!** By eating plants and fruits, primates shape the trees and bushes. They also spread plant seeds in their poo. Primate poo puts goodness into the soil and helps new plants to grow.

Macaque ⟶

## why is a slow loris slow?

A slow loris likes to take life at a gentle pace. Moving slowly saves energy, so you don't need to find lots of food. It also helps an animal to stay hidden from predators.

Slow loris

### Race

Have a slow race with a friend. The last person to finish is the winner!

## watch out bugs!

Slow-moving primates can creep up on their prey, such as insects, and pounce at the last second.

## when do monkeys fall out of trees?

When they get too greedy! Bird eggs are a special treat for primates. Smart birds build their nests on slender branches where monkeys can't reach them.

# How fast can a gibbon swing?

**Gibbons move faster than any other primate.** They can swing through trees at great speed — up to 56 kilometres an hour. Gibbons can cover up to 15 metres in just one swing.

Gibbons

Crab-eating macaque

# Do monkeys eat crabs?

Some monkeys will eat almost anything they can find! Crab-eating macaques live in swamps and they will grab crabs and frogs out of shallow water. Sometimes they just drop into the cool water for a swim.

# Do primates have hands and feet like us?

Instead of paws and claws, primates have fingers, toes and flat fingernails just like us. This means they can grab hold of branches and delicately pinch small things.

## count

If one macaque can catch five crabs, how many can three macaques catch?

## super movers!

Spider monkeys are some of the fastest primate climbers. They have very long arms, legs and tails.

# which monkey is the biggest?

**Male mandrills are the world's biggest monkeys.** They are also the most colourful of all furry animals. Mandrills have enormous fangs that can grow to nearly 7 centimetres in length. Males are twice as big as females.

← Mandrill

# Why do chimps pull faces?

Chimps pull faces to show how they are feeling. They pout when they want attention, open their lips when they are playful and bare their teeth when they are worried.

## Pout

Try out some chimp faces in front of a mirror. Make an angry face too.

Pouting face

Worried face

Play face

## Go wild!

Beautiful golden tamarins were once popular zoo animals, but now they are being released back into the wild so they can live free.

# Which monkey has a moustache?

Emperor tamarins have big white moustaches. Other tamarins have golden fur, crowns of white hair, beards or hairy ears. Tamarins live in South America.

# Do monkeys change colour?

**Silvered langurs do!** These monkeys have silver-grey fur, but their babies are born bright orange. After three months, grey fur begins to grow. No one knows why the babies are orange, but it may remind older monkeys to be gentle with them.

Silvered langur

Silvered langur baby

# which ape has a colourful bottom?

A healthy male mandrill baboon has a brightly coloured bottom. Their bald bottoms have blue, pink or lilac skin. Female baboons often have pink or bright red bottoms.

## A handy tail!

Monkeys use their tails like an extra arm or leg. They can hang from branches using their tails.

Sifaka

# why does a sifaka skip?

Skipping is a fast way for sifakas (a type of lemur) to travel. They stand upright, with their arms stretched out, and skip sideways, scooting across the ground. Sifakas stick their tails out so they don't fall over as they hop, bound and leap.

## Imagine

Pretend to be a sifaka and skip about!

# How big is a gorilla?

**Adult male gorillas are very big.** They are called silverbacks, and they are up to 180 centimetres in height and weigh about 300 kilograms. That's the same weight as almost four people!

Silverback gorilla

## Measure

Use a measuring tape to find out how tall a gorilla is.

# What is the ugliest monkey?

Red uakaris (say: wak-ar-ees) are one of the ugliest monkeys. When they are born, baby uakaris have grey faces, but they turn bright red as they get older.

## Bathtime fun!

Suryia the orang-utan lives in a wildlife park. He loved splashing in the bath and was taken to a pool. Suryia can now swim underwater!

Red uakari

# Why do gorillas beat their chests?

When a silverback gorilla stands up and beats his chest, it is time to get away fast! This is his way of warning you that he is getting angry and might attack.

# HOW do bonobos keep clean?

**Bonobos spend lots of time cleaning each other's fur.** They pick out bits of dirt, dead skin and even insects. This is called grooming and it is an important way for apes to make friends.

Bonobos

# Do baboons have manes?

Male hamadryas baboons have large manes of hair that make them look big. Ancient Egyptians thought the silver-white manes made the baboons look sacred, or holy.

## scoop and sip!

Some baboons dig holes by ponds and let water flow into them. The water is clean enough to drink, with no nasty bugs in it.

## Think

Can you think of any other animals that have manes of hair or fur?

# which orang-utan is in a film?

King Louie is one of the cartoon stars of a Disney film called *The Jungle Book*. He loves to sing, dance and play practical jokes. The story is based in an Indian jungle, but orang-utans don't really live in India.

King Louie

Baloo

# Which monkey has a big nose?

In Southeast Asia there are small monkeys with big noses. They are called proboscis monkeys (say: prob-os-kis), because proboscis is another word for 'nose'. The males have the biggest noses of all. When they run, their noses flop up and down!

Proboscis monkeys

## Make
Use card and coloured pens to create a monkey mask.

# Why do De Brazza's monkeys have white beards?

To scare other monkeys! De Brazza's monkeys also have long fangs. When they open their mouths wide, the white beards and long teeth make them look scary.

De Brazza's monkey

## Go ape!

Every year, people all over the world dress up as gorillas and run 7 kilometres. They raise money to save the few gorillas that still live in the wild.

# How do orang-utans stay dry?

Orang-utans live in tropical forests where it rains a lot every day. These clever apes use big leaves like umbrellas, and hold them over their heads to keep dry!

# HOW do monkeys keep warm?

**Most monkeys live in warm places.**
Japanese macaques live in mountainous
areas where the weather can turn very cold.
They keep warm by soaking in pools of hot
water that bubble up from the ground.

Japanese
macaques

Bushbaby

# Why do bushbabies leap?

Bushbabies leap to catch their prey. They are fast movers, and can even take scorpions and spiders by surprise. In just one leap, a bushbaby can cover 10 metres!

## Lucky for some!

Only some lucky Japanese macaques have hot springs to soak in. Others have to huddle together to keep warm when cold winds bring snow.

# Which primate has two tongues?

Bushbabies use two tongues to eat gum, which comes from trees. They use their teeth to scrape the gum from the bark, then wipe it off their teeth with the special second tongue.

# Quiz time

**Do you remember what you have read about monkeys and apes?** Here are some questions to test your memory. The pictures will help you. If you get stuck, read the pages again.

3. Why do chimps lick sticks?

page 8

4. Why does an aye-aye have a long finger?

page 11

1. Are gorillas scary?

page 5

5. When do baboons show off?

page 13

2. Which lemur has a stripy tail?

page 7

6. Why is a slow loris slow?

page 15

## 7. Do monkeys eat crabs?

page 17

## 8. which monkey has a moustache?

page 19

## 9. why does a sifaka skip?

page 21

## 10. what is the ugliest monkey?

page 23

## 11. Do baboons have manes?

page 25

## 12. which monkey has a big nose?

page 26

## 13. HOW do monkeys keep warm?

page 28

### Answers

1. Gorillas are usually gentle, but they can be fierce when they protect their families
2. The ring-tailed lemur
3. Because they get covered with termites when chimps poke them into big termite nests
4. To get to tasty grubs in trees
5. When there are females about
6. To save energy and stay hidden from predators
7. Crab-eating macaques do
8. An emperor tamarin
9. Skipping is a fast way for them to travel
10. The red uakari
11. Male hamadryas baboons do
12. The proboscis monkey
13. Japanese macaques keep warm by soaking in pools of hot water that bubble up from the ground

# Index